THE NAPKIN SERIES:

A THINKING MAN'S THOUGHTS AT THE BAR

ALAN DARY

outskirts
press

This book is for Ann.
The most supportive, loving and kind
human being I have ever known.

Preface

What the hell is a Napkin Series? Well you're about to find out!

During the course of its creation I described it to friends as a compendium of witticisms, verse and profoundities. But upon completion I realized that it has evolved into something much deeper. A journey of sorts. The witticisms are virtually non-existent, and anything profound remains to be seen. Thus, the bulk of the Napkin Series is verse. It has become an honest picture of the reflections of a thinking man faced with the first major dose of adversity in his life.

And the entire thing was written on napkins while sitting at the bar in various locations.

When the troubles actually began is a discussion unto itself. The docs would certainly say my issues started in childhood. But for the sake of the Series, my economic woes started in the late eighties, and the emotional duress followed. Up until 1988 I had established myself as a fairly successful individual in media management. I was up and coming as a young guy in the broadcast industry. I was respected in my profession, my community and among friends.

So what do I do? I try something new! I embark on a different career path. My reasons were numerous; suffice it to say it was that decision that started the economic woe that led to what I can now say was my (temporary) decline.

By the summer of 1991 I had no income, I was living in a virtual slum three family (albeit one that I owned) and was sharing my apartment with a friend. Quite philosophical, he was bright, introspective and also a down and dirty dyed in the wool alcoholic. I had no concept in what direction I wanted my life to go and I really lacked the motivation to determine what was next. In retrospect, I was depressed. But at the time I determined that the smart thing to do was visit my roommate daily at his place of work. (damn, I was brilliant!) He was a dishwasher at the local bar. It was there that the Napkin Series was born.

While sitting at the bar one day with my friend, I was doodling on a napkin (the only scrap paper at the bar). I asked my pal Billy his favorite word and jotted it down. Then I did the same with my own favorite word. The next logical step was to write down why they were our favorite words. And that became the very first napkin, and the series took on a life of its own. I made it a point to write napkins whenever I was out in a restaurant or bar/nightclub, etc. Some of the early entries reflected upon my new job as a clerk in a grocery store (written rather tongue in cheek). But quickly the verse turned to inner reflection and observations of people around me. Often they were of a dark nature. But I was dark. I was enmeshed in a black cloud and most often the blackness prevailed.

That, and mostly that, is what makes this Series so enlightening. A bright, thoughtful man who was gifted in so many ways literally sinks to the depths of depression and writes about it in both a direct and also metaphorical way. Sounds like a ball, doesn't it?

In looking back, it was a fascinating journey. I discovered sides of myself that I never knew existed. I recognized merit and worth in people I never dreamed was possible. And I survived. More importantly, I recognize that my ordeal was nothing compared to others who face decisions and events of mortality far more dire than mine. They say hind sight is 20/20. In looking back, the adversity I faced then was a mere blip compared to things in my future. Yet I also recognized that any ordeal, no matter how unimportant in the grand scheme of things, is HUGE to the individual living it. That recognition has given me empathy and tolerance.

My price was small. What a bargain.

Acknowledgments

I never understood the significance of acknowledgments in a book until I finished the manuscript for this book. There are so many people to whom I owe gratitude, and to a great many that I owe so much more! I apologize if I have overlooked you. So many have in some way shaped and affected my life that it would be impossible to name you all. To that end I offer a large and generic THANK YOU. I have chosen also to leave some names out if I felt that in some way it may divulge information about them that they would prefer to not be made public.

First and foremost, I thank God for the mixture of genetics and chromosomes and other scientific soup that has congealed to make me. I learned over the course of the Series how lucky and gifted I truly am. I have been given a myriad of gifts, and these gifts have opened up worlds for me to explore, learn and enjoy. My only regret is that I didn't recognize them sooner.

To the man with the 'mystery tears' (and somewhere, somehow) he knows who he is, I offer thanks for bringing me to the edge of alcoholism and trying to push me over while I looked into that abyss. Thanks also for an up close and personal look at that disease and his true nature. For that lesson, I owe a lifetime.

I have to thank Sue and Warren a million times over for opening their home to me; for allowing me to live in relative independence and for offering me a family whenever I wanted it. Its unfortunate that my upbringing never gave me the ability to fully express my gratitude (I'm working on it!). In the meantime, I hope this will suffice.

I offer the same level of thanks to Jim. It is his cash loans at that time that helped me through the early stages (and unbeknownst to him) helped pay for some of my visits to the local watering holes where napkins were created. I do and will owe him much more than just money that I paid back.

It would be outrageous if I didn't acknowledge TB. For at least one month she gave up sleep and time to answer those early morning door bells and offered me her couch and ear while I sat and stared or simply cried. She offered no advice, no consolation and no judgement. For that I will forever be indebted.

To my pal Laura, thanks for answering those many late night phone calls. Thanks for telling me I was a good person before I knew it, and thanks for letting me tell you when I did figure it out! The weather is here, wish you were beautiful.

Perhaps I should be most thankful for the Witch Doctor. She recognized my need and took me seriously. She offered support, she offered input, she pointed toward solutions. She never preached, she never judged and she never lied (kindly or otherwise). And she did it all because... well, I don't know why. But I do know that she spent hundreds of hours showing me that I can be my own parent and that I can fill the holes. Most importantly, she made me believe that you can connect your head to your heart. And after many years I am just beginning to tie the two together.

A man who has no idea how much he affected my life is one I must thank. Gramps. Uncle George. The Big Guy. These are but three of the monikers I have used for him. Our relationship was odd, one that few, if any, people really understood. Yet this is a man for whom I have the utmost respect and admiration. He is the person most responsible for my effort to "survive" and he didn't even know it. But it is his integrity and sense of honor that became my beacon. He treated me as well as he treated his own family. If my actions in any way can equal one tenth of the integrity he possessed, then I will consider myself a success. So rest assured Mr. M that at least one person on this planet has been greatly affected by what you are and what you represent. To coin an incredibly corny phrase, one that is truly heartfelt on part; thanks for being you George.

I would also be remiss if I didn't dedicate a major portion of these thank yous to Jack. Always accepting, never condemning, Jack never pried or asked why. And advice he did offer was done so with reticence and always in a constructive and acceptable manner. Jack showed me that anyone can become whole and have fun doing it. For yelling at me (twice), for laughing with me, for listening to me and for all the manual labor (never mind money and free meals!) thank you. And thanks most of all for your belief in me and for your friendship.

People and (or) their actions can affect us and shape us both in positive and negative ways. Lessons can often be learned 'the hard way'. So it is only fair that I include a very special thank you to my dear friend The House Stealer. It is through her that I learned a number of valuable lessons, a few of which deserve mention here.

The first is that dysfunction in the home of our upbringing can create evils and hatred and coping mechanisms far greater than any other force. But what amazes me the most is though the individual may occasionally recognize it, they're often powerless to change it. That evil becomes their greatest friend, and using it satisfies needs much greater than kindness or love ever will. I have also learned that one individual's dysfunction is another individual's weapon. Though the pain is the same, the utilization of such can manifest itself in entirely different behaviors. Therefore, never expect your opponent's actions to be predictable. Action born out of sickness is usually irrational.

And the last lesson that I learned from the ordeal with The House Stealer is a simple one. In any skirmish, no matter how large or small, the best defense is a strong offense. There is no strength or power in kindness in such affairs. Rage (from whatever source) will always overcome it. Thus, shoot first.

My final acknowledgment goes to a woman who probably doesn't even realize all the ways in which she helped me. Some are obvious, others subtle. The most important reason I need to thank her is because I realized through her actions that not everyone is able to look at themselves with an honest eye and some never will. Regardless of cost, sometimes its easier to close one's eyes when looking in the mirror. Personally, I am unable to do that and as a result I am becoming whole and healthy. She could not do that, and I believe will always feel a twinge of emptiness. She'll lash out at those she believes she loves, projecting her internal anger at them. And then she'll feel guilt and project some more. The mirror faces another mirror; one must step in between the two to break the perpetuity. By watching her fail to do that, I learned how. It cost us both dearly, but I'll benefit in the long run and that too requires a thank you.

A very special thank you to
Michael Conley of the
12 Ocean Grill for the cover photo setting.

Thanks to Traci DeSeve for setting up the above!

Thanks to Michael Neubert for
shooting the wonderful cover photo
and his input therein,

and a heartfelt thank you to
Rosalind Giuffrida Hartley for
translating the emotions on these pages into
the incredible artwork.

Bill's favorite words

1.) HEINOUS. Because so many people are

2.) LOATHSOME. Because so many people are

Uncle Al's fab favs

1.) VITUPERATIVE. Because everyone should be

2.) SYCOPHANT. Because most of them are

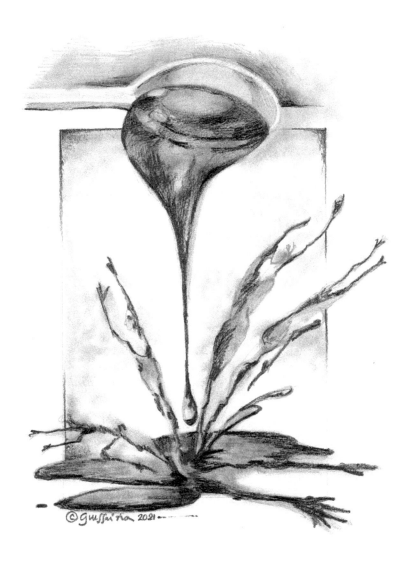

The spoon of life, it scoops and it probes
it investigates my innards
it separates my lobes.
It glistens and shines, this spoon of life,
it scrapes grey matter
it comes without strife.
But when its full and overflows its edges,
my hope drips to the floor
like old lover's many pledges.

So what is false and what is true?
Only the spoon of life
can answer that for you.

And there she sits across the bar.
Her head in hands, her mind so far.
Melancholy, unhappy, depressed.
She stands out loud among the rest.
A dirtbag she's not; or at least it appears
or is this just denial
of my many fears?

(ode to a bag boy)

The sky's the limit as he places the boxes under the cans.
Why do the idiots wear ties while I do this?
Can't they understand my artistic freedom is suppressed?
Don't they know that within their midst
stands a writer, a lawyer…
a brain surgeon with a twist?

Warped and distorted. Messed inside.
Paper or plastic? Is that what you hide?

I rise above or try so often.
I delude myself and live without caution.
I curse them all, nameless fools.
Yet I've broken them all. All their rules.
I'm one of them yet won't admit.
And that's the problem, that's really it.

Pick 'em pack 'em make sure they're ripe.
Water and mist like early morning dew.
Such strange dreams and thoughts we had.
Can you believe this is you

The fate of the driven
is determined by the extent of their obsession.
But their fate can only be learned
by the extent of their lesson.

Drink or not
the difference makes none.
You are the universe
You are one.

You know you love
you know you care.
Your love it lingers
you're just not sure where.

Explosions of emotion spew forth without provocation
Waves of pain roll over me like water of the ocean.
Tides of panic ebb and flow
Escape. It always comes so slow.

And when it does, I know it to be temporary.
Peace does not exist for those afflicted like me.
Therefore
peace does not exist.
Can't ya see?

So here he sits one week later.
Has he become a produce hater?
Does he have murderous visions of crushing cantelopes?
Is packing carrots out of his scope?
Are the important questions of life slipping him by?
Does he no longer care or wonder why?
And most of all
does he still cry?

The room has changed and so have the faces
but the angst is the same in all of these places.
We carry it with us from room to room
from birth to life and to the tomb.
Some are destined no matter how lucky they are
to travel always troubled on this journey so far.
Its the unfortunate truth
Its the inherent prize.
Its the thinking man's enigma
because he exposes the lies.

I remember and feel as if it was yesterday.
You looked at me in your very special way
you touched my hand, my arm, my heart.
You told me it was love
that we'd never part.

I gave you everything I had
and just like I thought
Once again its me
the one that's sad.

Sometimes it feels as if the slide seems to slow
as if all that pain will really go.
This is one of those moments when it seems to be
that pain and rot is almost out of me.
I know it'll be back. Of that I am sure.
And then again I wonder
is there really a cure?

The series continues and the mystery widens.
The thoughts abound. The book gets thicker.
Male or female...they're all the trickier.

I've become an almost middle aged man
with a bulge on the waist
looking at youth I can no longer taste.
From twenty to thirty the years flew by.
I was on top of the world. I didn't care why.
Well here I am
the pain is overwhelming.
I knew it would come
Yet let no one tell me.

Here among strangers where I don't belong
I wonder if I'll fit and if I'll be strong.
So judgmental are we who so hate to be judged.
Yet our stance is so firm it seems we'll never be budged.
But we continue to seek the key that we need
the key to contentment.
The key to succeed.

They mingle and mix
the facades they abound.
They're beautiful. They're pretty.
Yet they can't hear a sound.
Their oblivion is enviable
their ignorance is bliss.
Is that all there is?
Does it only come to this?

Each bend in the road
seems to throw another curve.
Just when the sailing seems smooth
you get what you deserve.
Just another mirror image
slaps you hard and fast.
The attitude you lost
is back from your past.

Life continues to amaze me
with its twists and with its turns.
With its subtleties and with its surprises
some of which I've been known to yearn.
Yet I carry on with laughter
with smiles and with hope
Knowing deep inside
I'm probably just a dope.

One can have the greatest tools
and still they're not enough
to deal with fools.
One can have the greatest logic
but sometimes even that
can't make it stick.

Some things in life you cannot change.
All the hope, all the prayers, all the pent up rage.
These things are futile
while you're locked in your cage.

The answer, it does exist
its just beyond your finger tips.
So stretch real hard and concentrate
Time is passing, but really
its not too late.

Why should we kill them
when we have enough pain?
Why seek situations
that to me are the same.

Do I not like myself
to that degree?
To inflict pain upon myself
the pain that you see.

I try so hard
but can't understand.
Can you help me out?
Give me your hand?

I was told that my face lit up
when I answered your call.
I find that so fascinating
I thought my response seemed so small.

The effect our encounter had
(so brief that it was)
goes far beyond normal expectation
Wonderin' why, or was it just because?

Is this meant to be
as we've often thought in the past?
Is this the time we're sure
that faith and trust can last?

Ya know, I sit in this bar
as I have many times before.
I can't understand the attraction
I know there are no surprises in store.
Yet I come back once again
to spend money I don't have
to sit and conjure rhyme
and wonder why I waste my time.

Am I looking for something
or am I just bored?
Is someone there to answer me
and could it be You, the Lord?

Often people make inane comments
ones that make no sense.
Comments born out of stupidity
comments I consider dense.
Just know that a mind that doesn't change
is sometimes a mind
that is filled with doubt
or intellect
or rage.

Being afraid to say hello
or fearing that I wouldn't measure up,
were thoughts so foreign to me
when it came to women I'd see.

But at this moment I encounter
yet another first in new emotions,
I sit and watch a woman
and I'm afraid I'll cause a commotion.

She seems to be so genuine
with unadulterated beauty.
Yet she's not someone I'll speak with
she's not someone I'll see.

Instead I'll watch from afar
while she sits really so near.
I'll contemplate and I'll stall
I'll give in to my newest fear.

Sadness permeates me and seems to overcome my soul
I don't know why.
I watch all the people seeming to have fun
All I wanna do is cry.

I continue to write
for the supposed book some day.
And wonder if it'll always
always be this way.

There are moments when I feel so lucid
when all my troubles and weakness fade back into the ground.
When the world seems so conquerable
whether or not you're around.

And then there are those moments when I feel so empty
when all my strength and energy slip back into the night.
When the world seems so lonesome
and fills me with all that fright.

I saw a man in the men's room
who's son can really sing.
He and his wife were here
because it was the only right thing.

I guess I've longed for that
but deep down know it cannot be.
My dad has never really known
or ever really cared for me.

So may that son truly understand
how blessed he'll always be.
And may that father know
the sight he has given me.

Take your passion and make it happen
that's what the song said.
I know its so true
yet its myself that I've misled.

My fears overcome my passion.
My pride it gets in the way.
I wanna do it I wanna take action
But I don't, and what can I say?

He makes me sick, he's such a dick.
that man sitting next to me.
The con is on, he's feelin' strong
Its disgusting she cannot see!

Finding the prey then losing the trail
another day goes by avoiding that wail.
Then fate intervenes, the prey reappears
You come to the brink you fight back the tears.
Stalking the victim plotting your plan
Feeling so broken, you're such an empty man.
Stalling for time to make your kill
Hoping by then you'll have lost your will.

Pain. Hidden by pleasure so unhealthy.
You try to look but cannot see.

Life. A journey so difficult to traverse.
The choices are many but the options are worse.

Growth comes slowly
sometimes not at all.
For others its quick
and for others it stalls.
The point is to take the steps to walk that road
to move toward health
to continually unload.

Creative or contrived
they flow from your pen.
Words that are conjured
suck them into your den.

Who does this writing?
Is it really you inside?
Or is it their response
and from that you hide?

Before you were never sure
but now the answer seems closer.
You've got to rebuild you
in small, lighthearted doses.

Never written here before
never even tried.
Can't say I'm confused
I surely know why.

Sluts and studs, playin' the game
Knowing deep down
I'm really the same.

I really hate them
one and all.
Does this mean I hate me?
'Cause I'm really having a ball.

Life's an adventure
that I know.
But its the smart ones
who know when to go.

The question lingers
how smart am I?
The answer may be known
or heard in a sigh.

They say I'm so much better off
than I was one year ago today.
But I think only the front has improved
'cause that's been my only way.

My insides keep screamin'
they don't know where to go.
I don't know who the hell I am
I don't know what to show.

Intimacy seems so far from my reach
so foreign and unknown to me.
Yet I long for it so often
Knowing its something I'll probably never see.

I'm not sure if I've ever really known it
I'm not sure I know what it is.
But I pray someday that I'll find it
to see it as more than a wish.

What a wretched existence.

Whose is more wretched? Mine or theirs?

It isn't a napkin
but it'll have to do
this piece of paper
on which I now write for you.

Its a new bar
different from the others.
The people are honest
they act almost like brothers.

They have no class
they have no money.
But they have lots of fun
and isn't that what counts honey?

I wonder if I'll ever really know
who it is who does those things.
The man who makes them laugh
The man who makes them sing.

Is it me or someone I've created?
Is it me, or someone that I've hated?
Or is it both, something I already know…
But I don't want them all to see,
don't ever want to show.

Life confounds me in spite of my brains.
It angers and elates
and most often causes pain.

The normal order this most certainly is not
but it's what was given
what my path hath wrought.

Another napkin and here we go.
is this one for real or is it for show?
Is this one from the heart
or do I even know?

I suppose it doesn't matter
because this one's for fun.
Its just another for the Napkin Series
long before its done.

Life's such a fucking mystery
yet I wouldn't change it a bit.
I really do love it
this pensive, critical shit.

© Griffiths 2021

Broken lives. They crack and mend
or so it seems.
But mending is fleeting
isn't it?
So it seems.

Talent, talent, oh fucking talent.
So many have talent.
Don't they have a clue
what it is that they can do?

It makes me cry
in a most literal sense.
It makes me wanna die
cuz I won't give myself a chance.

Talent. Talent. Oh fucking talent.

*Its been a dark day
it seems to be my way.
Inbred or learned
it really doesn't matter.
I'm probably just mad
MAD as a hatter.*

Everything is tarnished tonight
the magic is gone.
Nothing has seemed right
for seemingly oh so long.

Pervasive darkness/looking for a crack in the wall.
Pervasive light reaching another frustrating stall.
I wonder when it will end
when I'll hear the unheard call.

Voices filled with agony are somewhere inside
and they're screaming.
It's just that my ears have been closed
because I've been off somewhere dreaming.

But the dreams, they have never occurred.
You see, its my own voice that I've never heard.

We let go when there's nothing to hold
and we don't understand.
And when we do
we find we cannot.

Its as if I have crossed a thresh hold
a barrier I have created for safety and defense.
A wall of my own making
to ward off their demeaning intent.

Have I found the greatest love of all
and its inside of me?
Have I finally learned what's in me
and can I take my future moments
to look in and see?

Sometimes ya gotta let go
of your greatest fears
to gain the greatest love
of all your years.

Ya gotta finally believe
all that ya try not to.
Ya gotta finally give in
to the one you really want to.

The faces have changed
the rooms have changed
and even the napkins.
But the essence is all the same.
A constant battle for what is right
a constant battle, always a fight
to find what's in me.
To finally help me see.

I guess there are times when life seems so simple
and others when the answers just don't come.
And then there are times when I know the solution
can only come from the battles I've won.

Altered states of mind
achieved by many means.
Altered states of reality
never are what they seem.
Altered friendships
relationships gone awry.
Questioning everything all the time
making me just wanna cry.

I guess they really don't understand
and that's the hardest part.
They watch and listen and think they know
they participate
but it never shows.

The depths they can reach
they never, ever achieve.
All the dreams you've had?
Give up. Get up.
And leave.

So the barmaid at Luca's
says I better say nice things.
Does she mean about the way she serves
or about the way she sings?

Who really cares
and that's what counts.
And won't she shit
when this is published and out?

Our perceptions of others
are sometimes deceived.
Often our opinions are not
what we had once believed.

The difficulty is in knowing
and judging correctly...
the perceptions we've formed
off center, or directly.

If you can't change your mind, you probably don't have one.

Why is it so hard
to see who I am?
To stop asking questions
to forget where I began?

Can't I move on
with what I've been given?
Can't I enjoy it
this life that I'm livin?

I'm so gifted I know
yet I still can't believe.
When will this onslaught
finally give me reprieve?

Comfort zones come
with good friends or not.
Time is the only sure thing
that you know that you've got.

Or is it truly a friendship
that causes that warmth?
And not just the time factor
but something very much more?

I think I feel the holes filling
ever so slowly I see my choices unfolding.
I think I sense the fear of decisions
and it seems so lonely.
But this is what I wanted
so long ago
I hope the right answers
are the ones that I'll know.

What is it that happens
to make us reform
to make us change,
to become less forlorn?

What life altering moment
can there possibly be
to force a new reality,
to make me be me?

I stand at ocean side in darkness
to hear the waves crash in.
I wonder about the life out there,
the life around and within.

And now I sit at bar side
watching the fish in a tank.
Their life to me is exposed in there
but to whom should I turn to thank?

Their life is peaceful and quiet.
Contented, but sterile I think
while that woman sits across from me
looks over at me with a wink.

How curious that I compare
my life to that of the fish,
and interact with the woman who winks
who can offer nothing more than a wish.

And why do I need to thank someone
for letting me see the fish?
Can't I accept that I have foresight
the ability to think and accomplish?

And the man sitting next to me
hustles the recently married bar maid.
He says the only success in life
come from the risks we take.

So now I know to be open, to avoid sterility and confines.
to risk the wilds of nature, to act on those gut impulses of mine.

Kennedy, Kennedy and King.
Is it the KKK
or just an assassination thing?

I sit on the side and watch
the petty things and moods
that young lovers use
as weapons and tools.

If they only knew
the damage they cause.
The time that they waste
regardless of cost.

Thank God I'm beyond it
Thank God I can see.
Thank God I no longer do it
and thank God I am me.

It is with disdain
that we entertain in these rooms
these rooms infested with creatures
who it seems have crawled from tombs.

It is with hope
we embark on journeys expressing our bliss
showing the world
we're not all like this.

Music is the language of the universe
it transcends space and distance
it travels to those depths.
It carries messages and feelings
faster than words can convey.
It gets the point across
better than one can ever say.

Never again is what you swore the time before,
But you're on the edge once again.
But this isn't it
It isn't part of the plan.

My expectations are sometimes high.
Too high to reach unless you touch the sky.
But there are people I expect so little from
and they're the ones to get me down.
Today I learned these ridiculous things.

I sat here almost a year ago
to write these silly napkins.
I was looking for my hero
in all the places I've been.

So it was just yesterday
when I realized my mistake.
I recognized then that my hero
is inside me for heaven's sake.

Almost a day to the year since this confounded series started
A year filled with growth and realizations galore
A year filled with truth and promise and so much more.
I've gained some friends and lost a few
I've lost some old values and I've formed some new.
Yet your name keeps popping up like some ghost of my past
Like some horrendous mistake I've made, whose damage
continues to last.
I believed in you and my judgement thereof
and you turned and you fucked me
like some unrequited love.
I've owned up to my errors, my transgressions and losses
I've learned just what I can do.
I know my decisions are made from thought
not by whimsical notion like you.

The wishful thinker dreams all will change.
The worker trudges on
always willing to tinker.

We try to change the ways of the world at large.
Yet life moves on
no change, no charge.

The drone is endless, without leisure or song.
The thinker moves on
the worker trudges along.

Joyful moments are but brief and fleeting memories
far too few for the years
or for someone with the gifts I possess.
Yet this is the reality I have known
and this is the reality I see.
A world so full of wonder
just slightly out of reach for someone like me.

I wish for you
yet you no longer know I exist.
I dream of you
of the fantasies I wished.

My reality and yours
now so far apart.
Yet it seems moments ago
they were from one heart.

Its been so long since I've committed to paper
the churning waves of emotion;
the ones to discard
the ones to savor.

Is it lack of interest
or lack of thought?
Do the words only come
with the pain I've bought?

All of these pages were written in various lounges, bars and restaurants throughout southern New Hampshire around 1989 - 1992. The original iteration of this book noted the time of each notation as well as the venue name on every page. But that became far too cumbersome in the editing process.

In lieu of that, here's a list of some of the venues in which this book grew.

Luca's, Hampton
Carmichael's, Manchester
OK Parkers, Manchester
AJ's, Seabrook
Duffey's Tavern, Manchester
Uptown Tavern, Manchester
Fratello's, Manchester
Bananas, Portsmouth
Galley Hatch, Hampton
Widow Fletcher's, Hampton

There were many more. But time has made those without notations hazy (or lost completely) But for every bartender or bar patron who remembers some guy sitting there scribbling on a napkin or some scrap of paper, it was probably me!

CPSIA information can be obtained
at www.ICGtesting.com
Printed in the USA
BVHW032258070822
644003BV00007B/214

9 781977 256324